# Major League SOCCER

## Orlando City SC

John Bankston

Copyright © 2020 by Mitchell Lane Publishers. All rights reserved. No part of this book may be reproduced without written permission from the publisher. Printed and bound in the United States of America.

Printing      1      2      3      4      5      6      7      8

First Edition, 2020.
Author: John Bankston
Designer: Ed Morgan
Editor: Lisa Petrillo

Series: Major League Soccer
Title: Orlando City SC / by John Bankston

Hallandale, FL : Mitchell Lane Publishers, [2020]

Library bound ISBN: 9781680204827
eBook ISBN: 9781680204834

PHOTO CREDITS: Design Elements, freepik.com, p. 14 Porsche997SBS CC-BY-SA-4.0, APImages, newscom.com

# Contents

**Chapter One**
Florida Waits .................................................................. 4

**Chapter Two**
An Early Champ ............................................................ 10

**Chapter Three**
Playing the Game .......................................................... 16

**Chapter Four**
Orlando's Best .............................................................. 20

**Chapter Five**
Orlando Communicates ................................................ 24

What You Should Know ................................................ 28
Quick Stats .................................................................. 28
Timeline ...................................................................... 29
Glossary ...................................................................... 30
Further Reading .......................................................... 31
On the Internet ............................................................ 31
Index .......................................................................... 32
About the Author ........................................................ 32

Words in **bold** throughout can be found in the Glossary.

# Florida Waits

## CHAPTER ONE

For Florida's Major League Soccer (MLS) fans, 2002 was brutal. The state lost not one, but *two* teams. The Tampa Bay Mutiny and the Miami Fusion **folded**. It took fourteen years before they got another MLS team.

The new team would not play in Tampa or Miami. Instead, MLS chose Orlando. The Central Florida city is best known for theme parks such as Disney World, Sea World and Universal Studios, and dozens of smaller parks. Orlando is the No. 1 place to visit in the U.S. In 2017, it had more than 70 million visitors

Soccer is the world's most popular game. Almost 250 million people play the sport. A game like soccer trained Chinese soldiers 2,000 years ago. Japan also had a sport where a leather ball was kicked around. Greeks and Romans played a game like soccer. Sometimes, the ball was too big to be kicked. So players just kicked each other.

The game we know today started in England. The first match was probably played more than 1,800 years ago. It celebrated England's victory over the region of Italy. The celebration wasn't for a game. It was for a battle. A small group of soldiers had defeated invaders from Rome.

After the match in Derby, England, the game became a regular event. Not everyone liked it. In 1314, according to historians, British King Edward II said, "There is a great noise in the city caused by [chasing after] large balls, from which many evils may arise." He made playing illegal. This did not stop the game.

In most countries, the sport is called football. Players use their feet to move the ball. Despite being popular across the world, pro soccer took longer to catch on in the U.S. Lots of people played soccer. They just didn't watch it. Major League Soccer helped to change that.

## Chapter One

Major League Baseball has the best players in the sport. They are paid the most money. The game attracts the most fans. Sports like hockey, football, and basketball all have top **professional** leagues.

Soccer's major league began because of the World Cup. Every four years, a different country hosts the sport's most important **tournament**. Thirty-two different teams compete. The U.S. wanted to host. To do this, organizers had to create a top-level professional league.

The U.S. won the honor to host the World Cup in 1994. The rest of the world saw how popular the sport was in the country. More people attended that year's World Cup matches than ever before. Orlando soccer fans watched matches at the Citrus Bowl, a **stadium** seating 65,000. Two years later, the U.S. hosted the Olympic Games. Although the hosting city of Atlanta saw most of the action, soccer teams competed across the South, including at the Citrus Bowl.

Major League Soccer's first season was also held in 1996. Soccer fans had supported the World Cup and the Olympics by enthusiastic game attendance and TV viewership. At first, they didn't support the MLS. Teams played to half-empty stadiums. In less than ten years, the League lost $350 million.

In 2002, the U.S. reached the World Cup quarterfinals for the first time. Afterward, more fans started watching MLS games.

# Florida Waits

USA's Gregg Berhalter (*left*) leaps for a header against Germany's Miroslav Klose during the World Cup quarter-finals match in June 2002.

## Chapter One

Orlando City SC's Kaká (*left*) battles for control of the ball against New York City FC's Andrew Jacobson in March 2015.

By 2015, the average MLS game attracted over 21,000 fans. The League was more popular than ones in France or Brazil. Games were also shown on TV. That year, Florida's new team started playing. Many believed it would do well. Alan Fyall, a professor at University of Central Florida, told a reporter in 2018, "[Orlando]'s definitely a soccer city."

The MLS started with just 10 teams. Today there are 23. Orlando City SC was the 21st team. There are 20 teams in the U.S., and three in Canada. There will be new teams in Cincinnati, Ohio, in 2019, while Miami and Nashville, Tennessee, will field teams in 2020.

# Florida Waits

Teams compete in two divisions, the Eastern and Western. Orlando plays in the Eastern. Like other clubs, 17 games are played at home, and 17 away.

Regular season play runs from March–October. Then the top teams compete in playoffs.

When a team wins, it gets three points. A tie gives a team one point. There are no points for losses. At the end of the season, the dozen teams with the most points go on to the playoffs. Six teams are from the Western Conference, and six from the Eastern Conference. The last two teams compete for the MLS Championship in December. Orlando City SC fans hoped their team would go all the way. After all, Orlando City had done it before.

# Fun Facts

**1** In Orlando, the Citrus Bowl (now called Camping World Stadium) may host World Cup matches in 2026.

**2** Although the U.S. did not qualify for the 2018 World Cup, the MLS sent more players to the Cup than any other pro league in the world.

# An Early Champ

## CHAPTER TWO

The first season was incredible. It began with Orlando SC beating FC New York 3–0. It ended with a Final decided by penalty kicks. Orlando came out on top. The team won the championship!

For a new team, it was a miracle. For Orlando City's MLS fans, it's a great memory. The championship was won by the United Soccer League version.

Both the MLS *and* the USL Orlando SC teams are connected to Phil Rawlins. Born in England, Rawlins wanted to bring top-level soccer to the United States. After buying the Austin Aztex FC in 2008, he bought Orlando Pro Soccer USL from Steve Donner, a sports promoter, team owner, and manager.

In Texas, Austin Aztex FC games rarely attracted 3,000 fans. After Rawlins moved the team to Florida and renamed it Orlando City SC, almost 8,000 fans cheered its first game on April 9, 2011. Fan support stayed strong. Rawlins promised to bring Major League Soccer to Orlando.

Major League Soccer had already added a second team to New York. "It doesn't take away anything from our interest in Atlanta, or our interest in Florida at some point," MLS Commissioner Don Garber told reporters. "We need to be in the Southeast. The question isn't if, it's when."

Nine days before Thanksgiving, the MLS gave the city something to be thankful for. In 2013, Orlando was awarded a MLS team. Its first season would be in 2015.

The USL team moved to Louisville, Kentucky. It was renamed Louisville City FC. Most of the team's players remained in the USL. The coach who helped the USL Orlando City SC team win two championships and top its division three times stayed. Adrian Heath would be the new MLS team's Head Coach. He'd even be coaching his son, Harrison Heath, whose first pro soccer games were in Orlando.

Harrison Heath started his pro career in Orlando.

# Chapter Two

Orlando City SC's first MS game was on March 8, 2015. The crowd was huge. More than 62,510 watched at the Citrus Bowl. Once again the season opener was against New York—the New York City FC. It ended in a draw. Orlando's first win was on the road, beating Houston Dynamo 1–0.

The MLS and the USL teams had a lot in common. They both played in the Citrus Bowl. They shared a head coach and an owner. Both were nicknamed "the Lions." There were even former USL players like defender Luke Boden and midfielder Heath. As the season ground on, there was one huge difference. The MLS team was losing.

Luke Boden (*left*) takes the ball away from Columbus City midfielder Dilly Duka in September 2016.

# An Early Champ

Orlando's first season the team won 12 games and lost 14. Coach Heath was fired on July 6, 2016. Many of the players left, including Heath's son, Harrison. New coach Jason Kreis struggled. Orlando City only won nine games in 2016.

Lions' fans hoped the next year would be different. In 2017, Orlando City would be playing in a brand new stadium.

The place where a soccer team plays is called the home pitch. In the beginning, MLS teams shared their pitch. They played in football stadiums and baseball fields. Even today, New York City FC shares Yankee Stadium with the Major League Baseball team. The New England Revolution and the Seattle Sounders play on fields designed for football.

MLS wants new teams to have soccer-specific stadiums. Soccer superstar David Beckham was one of the Miami team's new owners. His fame didn't keep MLS from rejecting their first site.

"We can't go to Miami without the right stadium," Commissioner Garber told reporters. "David understands that. The city understands that. We can't have different rules for Miami than we'd have for any other city."

When Orlando City played at the Citrus Bowl, there were usually lots of empty seats. Even the loudest cheers were swallowed in the huge space.

# Chapter Two

The new downtown Orlando soccer stadium solved those problems. Close to many of the city's restaurants and nightclubs, it has a field eight feet lower than the street. Because the bottom portion has an open plaza, it lets anyone walking by see onto the field. The Orlando City Stadium, its website explains, was "designed with the intention of creating the loudest and most intimidating atmosphere in Major League Soccer." It also offers the only "safe-standing supporter" section for members of the team's fan clubs like the Iron Lion Firm and the Ruckus.

It would hold up to 28,000 people and cost $80 million. The field is all-natural grass. The stadium has a canopy to keep out the fierce summer sun.

Orlando City Stadium

# An Early Champ

Across MLS, home pitches range from 70 to 77 yards wide. They are between 110 and 120 yards long. Orlando City SC's new field would be one of the biggest in the League.

The new stadium didn't help. When the team first played at the Citrus Bowl, average attendance was over 32,000. During the team's first year there, it reached barely 25,000. Under head coach Jason Kreis, the Lions won just 10 games in 2017, and lost 15. The next year, after only 6 wins and 8 losses, Kreis was fired.

Fans hoped a new coach could help the team find its way. When Orlando SC hired James O'Connor as coach, they got more than a former player. They got someone who knew the team.

# Fun Facts

1. The team colors for home games are purple and gold. When the team travels, players wear purple and white for away games.

2. The logo shows the head of a lion in gold. Instead of a mane, the lion has 21 sun flares (because Orlando City SC was the 21st MLS team.)

# Playing the Game

## CHAPTER THREE

Road games are hard. Travel can be tiring. Players often don't get enough sleep, or eat right. Road games are even harder when the other team is a **rival**.

Orlando City's biggest rival was its closest team. Just a six-hour drive north, Atlanta United FC was also an **expansion** team that only started playing in 2017. Unlike Orlando, Atlanta made the playoffs. That July, the new team played the Lions at home. They sent a "gift." Near their stadium, a billboard promised: "Orlando, we're coming to conquer." They did. Orlando lost 1 to 0.

When Orlando traveled to Atlanta in September, United FC was leading the division. Orlando had won only one game since early July. They had lost eight.

Describing the differences in the teams, writer Charles Boehm explained, "[Atlanta] plays in a hulking, air-conditioned, retractable-roof [stadium]," while Orlando plays "in an intimate, noisy ground where the tropical sun beats down."

In soccer, the 12th player isn't on the field. They're in the stands. Fans help their hometown team with cheers and screams. That September 16th, more than 70,000 packed Atlanta's stadium. It was the highest-attended game in MLS history.

Orlando's Dom Dwyer scored two goals. Teammate Cyle Larin scored one. Only a single Atlanta player scored. Unfortunately for the Lions, Josef Martinez did it three times. That meant a tie game. Although Orlando has yet to beat its rival, players and fans feel their games show what SC can do. Just before their first meeting in 2018, Lions goalkeeper Joe Bendik told a reporter from the newssite, MLSSoccer.com, "Last year, we played them three times. All three of them felt like playoff games. [May 13th] is going to be an awesome opportunity for us."

Cyle Larin moves against Chicago Fire midfielder Razvan Cocis in July 2015.

Instead, Atlanta beat Orlando at home, 2–1. Midway through its fourth season, Orlando City hired its third head coach.

James O'Connor knew soccer. He also knew Orlando. The Irish player's pro career began with Stoke City FC in 1998. Founded in the 1860s, the English soccer team is the second-oldest pro club in the world. It also connected him to Florida.

## Chapter Three

Two years after O'Connor joined Stoke City, Phil Rawlins became a board member. He **recruited** the defender to play for USL's Orlando SC in 2012. The next year, O'Connor became a player-coach. In 2015, when the USL team moved to Kentucky, he became Louisville City FC's first head coach.

O'Connor helped the team win its first USL championship in 2017. The team also had the second most points in the League three years in a row. He hoped to help Orlando just as he helped Kentucky. Orlando had a problem. The team wasn't holding onto the ball. If players didn't have the ball, they couldn't score.

After a team loses the ball, the players' response can change the game. This part of play is called a "defensive transition."

"I think one of the things we spoke about is defensive transition," O'Connor told a reporter from *Pro Soccer* USA. "We're capable of scoring goals. At times we're guilty of giving the ball away very cheaply that's something we want to stop."

The coach wanted his players to keep the ball. He wanted them scoring. Although the team wasn't winning Pro Soccer writer Jordan Culver explained, "There's a different feel to Orlando City's attack these days." In three matches, Orlando scored first in two of them. In the 17 games played before O'Conner arrived, they only scored first in two of them.

Orlando City SC's struggles show how challenging soccer can be. One reason so many kids play is because it's easy to learn. The basics are simple. So is the equipment. It's a game played in backyards and parks. The rules rarely change.

## Playing the Game

There are eleven players per side. Goalkeepers are the only players allowed to use their hands. The rest of the players line up in a 4-4-2 formation. Four are in a line. Behind them are four more players. The last two stay close to the other team's goal.

Defenders stay closest to their own team's goal. They try to keep the other side from scoring. Midfielders divide their time from the middle of the field. The four players can defend or attack.

Defending midfielders move the ball away from their team's goal. Attacking midfielders send the ball toward their opponent's goal. Because they have to keep the ball in play, they usually have it more than the other players. It's a demanding position. The team leader or captain is often the center midfielder. The two forwards try to send the ball into their opponent's goal. Substitute players can be called in from the bench. Each team gets three. Players who are subbed out can't go back out to the field.

Soccer has two halves, 45 minutes each. The clock doesn't stop during pauses in play. As Orlando City SC's season moved past the halfway mark, fans hoped new players would change the team's future.

## Fun Facts

**1** The team mascot is a lion. The Orlando City SC team is also called "the Lions."

**2** Orlando City SC'S mascot is named Kingston. According to his bio, he's 6'7" with dreadlocks and weighs 210 pounds.

# Orlando's Best

## Chapter Four

Expansion teams are like the new kid at school. Other teams know each other. They've traveled to their stadiums. Their players are familiar. Expansion teams face the unknown.

In other sports, expansion teams often play poorly their first season. When the New York Mets joined Major League Baseball in 1962, crosstown rivals the Yankees won the World Series. The Mets record? Forty wins and 120 losses. The Tampa Bay Buccaneers had an even worse first year. When they joined the National Football League they lost all 14 games. The records for expansion hockey and basketball teams aren't any better. Across all four sports, most expansion teams lose more games than they win in their first year.

In 2018, the Las Vegas Knights reached the Stanley Cup Finals. The hockey team lost to the Washington Capitals. It was one of the best results for an expansion team in pro sports history. In Major League Soccer, one team did even better. In 1998, the Chicago Fire won both the MLS Cup and U.S. Open. The Fire was added to the original ten MLS teams alongside the Miami Fusion. The Fusion only played four seasons.

Orlando City SC hoped to be more like the Fire and less like the Fusion. In the USL, Orlando tied against higher-level MSL teams. Upon joining MLS, the team proved it was serious by hiring one of the world's best soccer players. Brazil's top attacking midfielder, Kaká, would earn $7 million. No other MLS player made as much money in 2015.

### Kaká (Ricardo Izecson dos Santos Leite)
**Attacking Midfielder** (2015–2017)

With 75 appearances and 24 goals, the player known as Kaká was the highest-paid player in MLS history, earning more than $7 million a year. In his first season he helped Orlando City advance to the quarter-finals of the Open Cup. He also earned the Most Valuable Player in the MLS All-Star Game. He retired after the 2017 season.

Kaká takes a free kick against the Portland Timbers in April 2016.

# Chapter Four

### Kevin Molina **Midfielder** (2015-2016)

The very first player signed to Orlando SC new MLS team, Molina had been playing for the USL version since 2011. After finishing his time at the USL with his 20th goal and his third Commissioners Cup in four years, he was looking forward to playing in the MLS. Unfortunately, the season had barely begun when an injury left him unable to play for the rest of the year. The next year, he scored his first goal for the MLS team helping the Lions win against the Portland Timbers 4–1. He went on to score ten more goals for the team, before being traded to Minnesota United.

### Joe Bendik **Goalkeeper** (2016-)

Although the sixty goals scored against him during his first year was the highest in MLS, he was popular because he played every minute of every game. He also made 114 saves his first year and has over 300 to date. He has won a number of the MLS "Save of the Week" contests. In 2018, he tied former USL Orlando City SC goalkeeper Miguel Gallardo's 81 appearances.

Joe Bendik

## Orlando's Best

### Dom Dwyer Forward (2017-)

Traded to Orlando from Sporting Kansas, Dwyer scored two goals against Atlanta on September 16th. The million-dollar player made 15 goals in 29 appearances. He also scored a goal in the second half of the 2017 MLS All-Star Game against Real Madrid.

### Harrison Heath Midfielder (2015-2016)

Although he only made five starts in six games, Heath was well known as the 18-year old son of Orlando City Coach Adrian Heath. The English player is once again playing for his dad, this time at Minnesota United FC.

## Fun Fact

Orlando City SC team had five players from Europe, six from South America and one from Africa. Sixteen players were born in the United States. Two came from Canada.

# Orlando Communicates

## CHAPTER FIVE

Joining an MLS team usually means leaving home. Players have to find a place to live. They have to learn how to get around their new city. It's even more challenging when it's not just a new city. For many MLS players, it's a new country as well.

Every team can have up to eight **international** players. MLS teams used to load up on European stars near the end of their career. Today, many MLS are younger players from South America and Central America. In Orlando, that has included Darwin Cerén from El Salvador and Bryan Róchez from Honduras. One of the team's biggest stars, Kaká, came from Brazil. In 2018, the team signed nineteen-year old Josué Colmán from Paraguay. "There are thousands and thousands of talented [players] in South America that are just waiting for an opportunity," Vancouver Whitecaps head coach Carl Robinson told *Sports Illustrated* in 2018. "These players want to be coached. They love football. And I want to work with players like that, because they know the game. I'm certainly excited by young, Hispanic players."

Past seasons have included players like Iraq's Justin Meram. Although he left midway through the 2018 season, Lamine Sané from Senegal and Middle Eastern players Libya's Mohamed El-Munir and Egypt's Amro Tarek added to the international roster.

In 2018, Orlando City had players from 10 countries, including the U.S. Coach Guillermo Sánche told a reporter from Pro Soccer USA.com, "It's important for them to get to know each other so any type of communication can flow better."

Not knowing the language is tough. But when players work to get along, it can overcome obstacles. Part of being on a team is helping each other out.

Justin Meram fights for the ball against Montreal Impact midfielder Samuel Piette in June 2018.

## Chapter Five

Defensive midfielder Uri Rosell was born in Spain. Today he can speak four languages including English. Although he's a new player himself, ever since joining the Lions in 2018 he works hard to help his teammates. In early May 2018, he told writer Jordan Culver, "If you can help them to feel more comfortable on the field it's very good to know and try to help them. With the Spanish guys, sometimes we say, 'You just have to speak English now.' They are trying. I know it's difficult." Added Midfielder Sacha Kljestan, "I think, for the most part, most guys here can understand English, which is important."

Still, it helps when English-speaking players learn a few words in another language. "Switching" the field, is *cambio* in Spanish. There are also Lions players who speak French, like Ludovic Lamine Sané, the 6'3" defender from Villenueve-sur-Lot, France.

Sacha Kljestan with New York Red Bull's Aurelien Collin in March 2018.

## Orlando Communicates

As the team faces its fourth losing season, players hope that working on communication will help them win. In soccer, the team is often only as good as its weakest player. Orlando has struggled to get more than one or two goals per game. Other teams often get four or more. To reach the playoffs, every player must pass and defend well. One mistake is often all it takes.

Facing a July 26th match against New York FC, forward Chris Mueller told writer Hannah Drosdick, "It's demanding for sure. All the guys need to be ready. It's been like that for quite some time now, just having to give your everything and be prepared." Although the Lions lost that game, it was to one of the League's top teams. Some saw reason for hope. The players were communicating better. The team was developing.

Lions fans remain hopeful. Many of them used to watch the USL team. Now that Orlando has its own MLS team, the teammembers must prove they belong in the highest level-league level in the country.

## Fun Fact

In 2018, Orlando City SC had international players from Venezuela, France, Egypt, Peru, Switzerland, Paraguay, and Libya.

# What You Should Know

- Soccer is the world's most popular game. Almost 250 million people play the sport.

- A soccer-like game was used to train Chinese soldiers 2,000 years ago.

- The game as it is now played probably started in England over 1800 years ago. It celebrated a victory in battle over invaders from Rome.

- Most people in the world call the sport football except in the United States, Canada, Japan, Korea, and Southeast Asia.

- People walking by the team's stadium can look in and see the field from the street.

- Orlando pro soccer teams have been named the Lions for more than 30 years.

- The highest-paid player in the MLS was on the Orlando City SC team in 2015. Brazil's Kaká was paid more than seven million dollars.

- There's a section of the Orlando City SC stadium where supporters can stand and cheer.

- The team's mascot is Kingston, a tall, muscular lion with dreadlocks.

## Quick Stats

**2015** U.S. Open Cup Quarterfinals
**2016** U.S. Open Cup Round 16
**2017** U.S. Open Cup Round Four
**2018** U.S. Open Cup Quarterfinals

# Orlando Soccer Timeline

**1875**    Orlando, Florida is founded with less than 100 residents.

**1964**    Central Florida's Orange Soccer Club is formed.

**1968**    Central Florida Soccer League is formed. By 2018 it will have over 110 teams and 2,500 members.

**1975**    The University of Central Florida Knights Men's Soccer team begins playing.

**1985**    A professional soccer team called the Orlando Lions is first formed.

**1990**    The Lions enter the American Soccer League.

**2010**    Orlando City SC (nicknamed "the Lions") is founded. The team will play in the United Soccer League.

**2013**    Major League Soccer officials announce they will expand to Orlando.

**2015**    With a different team but the same name, the Orlando City SC Lions begins playing in the MLS.

**2016**    Head Coach Adrian Heath is fired. Jason Kreis takes over. The team finishes the season with a record of nine wins and 11 losses.

**2017**    Missing the playoffs for the third season in a row, Orlando City ends the year with a record of 10 wins and 15 losses.

**2018**    Coach Jason Kreis is fired midway through the season, replaced by former USL Orlando City player James O' Conner. By late August the team had matched the previous year's record of 15 losses with 10 games left to play.

# Glossary

**expansion**
In sports, an expansion team is one added to a league's original line-up

**folded**
In soccer, it's when a team stops playing forever

**international**
Players who come from other countries

**professional**
Performing a job for money

**recruiting**
Getting someone to play for your team

**rival**
Team competing with another for the same goal

**stadium**
A large arena for sports like soccer

**tournament**
A competition with contests between many teams until one team is the final winner

## Further Reading

Crisfield, Deborah. *The Everything Kids Soccer Book*. Simon and Schuster. 2013.

Lock, Deborah. *Soccer School*, DK Publishing. 2015.

Killion, Ann. *Champions of Men's Soccer*. Philomel Books: 2018.

Nagelhout, Ryan. *Soccer: Who Does What?* Gareth Stevens Publishing, 2018.

Wahl, Grant. *Masters of Modern Soccer Crown*. 2018.

Woods, Mark. *Goal! Soccer Facts and Stats*. Gareth Stevens. 2011.

## On the Internet

**Beginners Guide to Soccer. U.S. National Soccer Team Players.**
https://ussoccerplayers.com/beginners-guide-to-soccer

**Kingston (Orlando City's Mascot)**
https://www.orlandocitysc.com/fans/kingston

**Orlando City SC**
https://www.orlandocitysc.com

**Orlando City SC Players**
https://www.orlandocitysc.com/players

**Soccer Positions**
ducksters.com, http://www.ducksters.com/sports/soccer/positions.php

# Index

| | |
|---|---|
| Atlanta United FC | 16-17, 23 |
| Bendik, Joe | 17, 22 |
| Berhalter, Greg | 7 |
| Boehm, Charles | 16 |
| Boden, Luke | 12 |
| Cerén, Darwin | 24 |
| Citrus Bowl (Camping World Stadium) | 6, 9, 12, 13, 14 |
| Colmán, Josué | 24 |
| Culver, Jordan | 18, 26 |
| Donner, Steve | 10 |
| Drosdick, Hannah | 27 |
| Dwyer, Dom | 17, 23 |
| England | 5, 10, 23, 28 |
| El-Munir, Mohamed | 25 |
| Florida | 4, 8, 11, 17, 29 |
| Gallardo, Miguel | 22 |
| Garber, Don | 11, 13 |
| Heath, Adrian | 11, 13, 23, 29 |
| Heath, Harrison | 11, 12, 13, 23 |
| Kaká (Ricardo Izecson dos Santos Leite) | 8, 21, 24, 28 |
| Kljestan, Sacha | 26 |
| Klose, Miroslav | 7 |
| Kreis, Jason | 13, 15, 29 |
| Larin, Cyle | 17 |
| Louisville City FC | 11, 18 |
| Louisville, Kentucky | 11 |
| Major League Soccer | |
|   history of | 5, 6 |
|   rules | 9, 18 |
| Martinez, Josef | 17 |
| Meram, Justin | 25 |
| Miami, Florida | 4, 8, 13 |
| Miami Fusion | 4, 13, 20 |
| Minnesota United | 22, 23 |
| Molina, Kevin | 22 |
| Mueller, Chris | 27 |
| New York City FC | 8, 12, 13, 26, 27 |
| O'Connor, James | 15, 17, 18, 29 |
| Olympics (1996) | 6 |
| Orlando, Florida | 4, 6, 8, 11, 12, 14, 27, 29 |
| Orlando City SC (MLS) | |
|   history | 8, 10, 11-12, 28, 29 |
|   record | 9, 12, 13, 17-18, 27 |
| Orlando City Stadium | 14, 15, 16, 28 |
| Rawlins, Phil | 10, 11, 18 |
| Robinson, Carl | 24 |
| Róchez, Bryan | 24 |
| Rosell, Uri | 26 |
| Ruckus | 14 |
| Sánche, Guillermo | 25 |
| Sané, Lamine | 25, 26 |
| Stoke City FC | 17, 18 |
| Tarek, Amro | 25 |
| United Soccer League (USL) | 10, 12, 21 |
| World Cup | 6, 7, 9 |

# About the Author

During my time in Portland, Oregon, I knew when the Timbers had a home game. Fans from the Timbers Army gathered everywhere. Those games created a parade. During the 2014 World Cup, the celebrations spread throughout the soccer-loving city. Fans arrived sporting the colors of just about every team that qualified. This is what I love about soccer. For me, the most interesting part of a game is how fans and teams relate to one another. The way fans are honored, even celebrated in soccer seems to be unique in sports. That spirit shows in the dedication of Orlando soccer fans who have stuck with their teams through so many dramatic changes. Because I live in Miami Beach and have spent a lot of time in Central Florida, I was extra curious about this new Orlando attraction. —**John Bankston**